Introduction

Introduction

"Endings are not only part of life; they are a requirement for living and thriving, professionally and personally. Being alive requires that we sometimes kill off things in which we were once invested, uproot what we previously nurtured, and tear down what we built for an earlier time. Refraining, giving up, throwing away, tearing down, hating what we once cherished—all are necessary."

Henry Cloud
Necessary Endings: The Employees, Businesses, and Relationships That All of Us Have to Give Up in Order to Move Forward

My inspiration to write this book came from Dr. Henry Cloud's idea that one of the most important things we can do in life is learn to be good at endings.

In the more than 25 years that I've worked closely with entrepreneurs, I've found myself having this really difficult conversation with business owners and team leaders time and time again—what to do when team members are no longer thriving in their work environment after you've tried everything.

This particular issue is near to my heart because I know the power of teamwork. With the right people in the right places, a team can leverage you in countless ways.

What I don't think people realize is how harmful it can be to have someone on the team who is not fully engaged, committed, or confident in their role.

A particular danger arises when people in your company are working only for their reasons and are not in alignment with you or your values. This has the potential to cause enormous damage because these people have the ability to negatively impact team morale and revenues. They can also leave a negative impression on your clientele.

This book is meant to give you context for how to confidently assess whether someone is a right fit for your company, and, if they're not, how to take action assertively.

In the words of Dan Sullivan, "The problem is never the problem; the problem is not knowing how to think about the problem." This book is about how to think about the problem of wrong-fit team members.

Letting go of team members is hard. It's my goal to help you rid yourself of any fear, guilt, or embarrassment you might be holding onto and to feel certain in your decision to let go of team members who are not aligned with or supporting your bigger future.

It's important that your business, which you've worked so hard to build, is always healthy and growing—and that you accept that sometimes you need to prune away to encourage new growth.

This is the power of *multiplication by subtraction*.

"Shannon Waller decisively explores an entrepreneurial breakthrough that other books never mention: strategically firing energy-draining employees for the specific transformative purpose of acknowledging and multiplying the outstanding contributions of those who always show up energized and committed."

Dan Sullivan
President & Founder, Strategic Coach

"Going through the discomfort of letting someone go and then having your staff ask you, 'What took you so long?' is embarrassing. This book has made me realize how important it is and how much easier it is for everyone involved to act quickly when there is doubt."

Mark W. Miller
Visionary & President, Performance Industrial

"This is not the book you read and retire to the shelf. I now have it available as a handy reference for hiring, maintaining, and letting go of team members. Shannon has provided a concise and clear what-to-do manual when faced with the challenge of letting go of employees. It provides thinking tools to build confidence and to end the procrastination that haunts us all in these difficult and emotional situations."

John Colaruotolo
President, Anco Builders

"I wish I'd had this book 20 years ago! I felt like it validated and gave me permission to follow my instincts and make some difficult but necessary endings. It gave us a lot to think and reflect on in our company's practices, both in how to handle existing personnel and how to be alert to new hires."

John Bews
President, Davis Bews Design Group Inc.

"Shannon has worked with so many entrepreneurs; she knows what we need—and how to give it to us. I love her checklist and takeaways. Multiplication By Subtraction gets to the point and will help me fix looming problems before they get out of hand. It will be a great guide the next time we need to prune the branches of our organization to prepare for future growth."

David Kolbe
CEO, Kolbe Corp

"The book is another fabulous addition to my team tool chest. I have already shared it with key people and used it as part of our evaluation and feedback method. What a great tool to reinforce the concepts of The Team Success Handbook. Another winner—love it!"

Dr. Katrin Schmidt
Entrepreneur & Veterinarian, Simcoe Veterinary Hospital

"Facing the reality of poorly performing team members isn't fun, but avoiding it is almost always costly. Shannon's experience dealing with these situations comes through in Multiplication By Subtraction. It's a great, practical resource for correcting problems while they're still correctable, as well as for ending them when necessary. This guide is a must-read for all entrepreneurs and their leaders!"

Amy Bruske
President, Kolbe Corp

"I love it. It's so true. I wish I had this book 15 years ago. I read it and think, 'That's me!' every time."

Stan Doobin
Job Title, Harvard Maintenance, Inc.

"Thank you, Shannon, for sharing your powerful concept of 'multiplication by subtraction.' It has allowed me to break loose and move on from wrong-fit team members. I am so grateful for your guidance, coaching, and commitment to the plight of entrepreneurs."

Terry Powell
Founder & Visionary, Franchise Source Brands International

Printed in Toronto, Canada. December 2016. The Strategic Coach Inc., 33 Fraser Avenue, Suite 201, Toronto, Ontario, M6K 3J9.

This publication is meant to strengthen your common sense, not to substitute for it. It is also not a substitute for the advice of your doctor, lawyer, accountant, or any of your advisors, personal or professional.

Library and Archives Canada Cataloguing in Publication

Waller, Shannon, 1965-, author
        Multiplication by subtraction : how to gracefully let go of wrong-fit team members / Shannon Waller with Jayne Stymiest.

ISBN 978-1-897239-49-0 (softcover)

        1. Employees--Dismissal of. 2. Teams in the workplace--Management. I. Stymiest, Jayne, 1989-, author II. Title.

HF5549.5.D55W35 2017   658.3'13   C2016-907788-8

This book is dedicated to successful entrepreneurs who have struggled to let go of a team member who just doesn't fit.

A special acknowledgment to Dr. Henry Cloud: Your book *Necessary Endings* was the inspiration for this one. It was the motivation I needed to create *Multiplication By Subtraction*, a conversation crucial to entrepreneurial growth. Thank you for helping us accept and know when to graciously cut ties with the relationships that are no longer helping us grow.

I'd also like to thank Babs Smith for coining the term "multiplication by subtraction" and thus naming this book.

With sincerest gratitude.

"There's a trick to the Graceful Exit. It begins with the vision to recognize when a job, a life stage, a relationship is over—and to let go. It means leaving what's over without denying its validity or its past importance in our lives. It involves a sense of future, a belief that every exit line is an entry, that we are moving on rather than out."

Ellen Goodman
Pulitzer Prize-Winning Journalist

Contents

Part 1 The Transformative Power Of A Right-Fit Team

Chapter 1
Why A Right-Fit Team?

The sustainable success of any entrepreneurial company centers on creating a right-fit team. Having the right people leverages you and frees you up to use your unique talents to build a viable, growing company.

Right-fit team members are engaged and knowledgeable, and spend the majority of their time working in the areas they're most passionate about and skilled at. When we talk about "right fit," we mean team members that fit with you, fit with each other, and fit with your unique entrepreneurial culture.*

A right-fit team:
- **Maximizes momentum.**
- **Eliminates friction and drag.**
- **Keeps and attracts the best talent.**
- **Provides a superior customer experience.**
- **Operates at a high level of teamwork and communication.**
- **Decreases frustration and increases fun.**
- **Encourages creativity and resourcefulness.**
- **Learns from mistakes and breakdowns.**
- **Constantly improves systems and processes.**
- **Leverages and frees up its members to do their best work.**
- **Commits to the long-term.**
- **Feels optimistic about the future.**
- **Aligns with your purpose and values.**
- **Increases productivity and profit.**

*For more information about helping your team cultivate an entrepreneurial attitude, please read *The Team Success Handbook: 12 Strategies For Highly Productive Entrepreneurial Teams.*

With a right-fit team, everything runs smoothly, your time and energy are freed up so you can focus on results, and you'll accomplish more than you previously thought possible.

You'll recognize right-fit entrepreneurial team members by the attitudes they display and the results they create. Use the following criteria to think about your current team members.

Are they ...

- [ ] **Accountable and responsible for results?**
- [ ] **Delighting clients?**
- [ ] **Increasing referrals and sales?**
- [ ] **Promotable and self-managing?**
- [ ] **Motivated and have "batteries included"?**
- [ ] **Operating according to a growth mindset?**
- [ ] **Delivering peak performance?**
- [ ] **Happy to provide leadership and increase efficiency?**
- [ ] **Demonstrating teamwork and decreasing stress?**
- [ ] **Taking ownership?**
- [ ] **Creative rather than reactive in unexpected situations?**
- [ ] **Passionate about helping other team members develop and grow?**

We've included our **Right-Fit Team Member Scorecard** on the back cover of this book to help you identify and score team members. Where do they fall on the scale? What does this mean for your company as a whole?

The caliber of your team will set you apart as an entrepreneur. It will make your company a more fun, productive, and engaging place to work. It creates a culture where people can find meaning in their work. Your team can take pride in their contribution to making progress on a shared vision that you're all committed to. Your right-fit team allows everyone greater freedom to do what they do best and for others with complementary talents to do the rest.

Now, to make it clear how this kind of team differs from what many people settle for, let's talk about the impact of having a wrong-fit person on the team. Below are some experiences leaders we've worked with described having.

Wrong-fit team members:
- **Have a negative impact on your credibility.**
- **Leave bad impressions with clients/customers.**
- **Consistently bring down the team's morale and interfere with a healthy company culture.**
- **In a leadership role, leave their team feeling unsupported or that their work is never good enough.**
- **Leave messes and expect others to clean them up.**
- **Train other team members in their bad habits.**
- **Are often involved in staffing issues and conflicts.**
- **Make small issues become crises because of their lack of transparency.**
- **Create friction and drag, slowing down projects, teamwork, and results.**
- **Cause you to lose right-fit team members.**

If you've ever worked with even one wrong-fit team member, just reading this list might make you queasy. Often, these behaviors are not visible to you as a leader. Some people are remarkably adept at putting up a good front. However, the people who work more closely with them are well aware of what's not working but are uncomfortable speaking up.

Often, though, these behaviors and the attitudes underlying them are noticed, but nothing is done. It's easier to sweep a problem under the rug than deal with it.

You'll want to take action sooner if you realize the lasting damage it may be causing your company or the opportunity cost of failing to handle the situation. Even one team member who is creating this kind of disruption can be remarkably toxic to an organization and its success. Not taking action encourages mediocrity because it becomes clear to everyone that you're willing to settle. When you do take action, you'll be a hero to your team. Setting and upholding standards builds trust and gives your team confidence in your leadership.

Throughout this book, you'll learn tools to assess who's a right fit for your company and who isn't. I'll give you a way to think about multiplication by subtraction with confidence so you can take constructive action and ensure your company is healthy and maximizing its potential.

TAKEAWAYS
The caliber of your team will set you apart as an entrepreneur.

Chapter 2
Why Subtraction Matters

Identifying the criteria for a right-fit team member for your company is an important first step toward developing a healthy organization. This provides a framework for assessing and diagnosing any problems, and taking effective action to continually develop the best, most creative, most productive team with which to build your company's future—a team that thrives.

But what happens when someone doesn't fit? How do you think about it? How do you handle it?

Too often, I've watched business owners and team leaders avoid this issue and live with the status quo for too long. This is where there's potential for enormous harm to be done without your even realizing it.

I've witnessed the negative impact a single individual can have on the entire organization too many times to count. Not only have I watched it occur within Strategic Coach®, but with numerous entrepreneurial clients I've worked with as well.

In a memorable Strategic Coach Team Leader workshop I was coaching, a participant shared the following story:

"We'd recently hired someone to take over the Client Service Manager role at our company. This was a really exciting deci-

sion for us, and the person we hired for the job was extremely intelligent and experienced.

My entrepreneur and I had, up to this point, been handling the role ourselves. We were really excited to be freed up, especially since the service side of our business occupies more than half of our time.

For the first 90 days, everything ran smoothly; he was savvy enough to play nice. But shortly after, the cracks started to show. Critical tasks weren't handled, and he became quite antagonistic, especially when it came to being held accountable. He believed he was indispensable, and this made him really hard to work with. I think we also let him get away with more than we normally would have because we so desperately wanted to free up some of our time. We gave him the keys to the castle way too soon.

These weren't the only problems, either. He was irresponsible with his time, dishonest, and would tell us things were done when they weren't.

He was better with clients, but we know now that it was because he was performing and trying to look good. He wasn't actually focused on or sensitive to our clients' needs.

It was after our "multiplication by subtraction" conversation in the workshop that I realized I needed to let him go. Hearing other people in the room state that the cost of keeping someone on board who's not the right fit is

far higher than letting them go confirmed my gut feeling. When I came to terms with the fact that the fallout wouldn't be as bad as I'd feared, I knew what I needed to do. I mentally committed to letting our new Client Service Manager go within the next 90 days.

Ironically, as I was about to board the plane after leaving the workshop that day, I received an email from one of our partners. He suggested I check in with one of our mutual clients due to some potential 'issues.' As far as I knew from our Client Service Manager, everything was fine. It was an interesting way to start a three-hour flight—this email staring me in the face and all that time to worry about what had gone wrong.

When I got back to the office the next day, I communicated my thinking to my entrepreneur, giving him a rundown of the recent issues and my decision to let our Client Service Manager go within the next few months. He asked me why we needed to wait. Why couldn't we let him go tomorrow? My heart sank to my feet; I knew he was right. I was giving myself all the typical excuses to delay what I knew was going to be a very difficult conversation.

After we got everything in order, we finally had the courage to let him go. He was angry and pushed back, as was expected, but we knew short-term pain was better than long-term.

Shortly after, we made sure to connect with our top five clients to communicate the recent change. Independently, they all expressed the same sentiments: They could tell he wasn't the right fit for our company. Had we waited to let him go, there's no question we would have lost some of our clients.

Looking back, there were a few clues that hinted at his misalignment. Our office manager was having a hard time working with him, and it was clear that a lot of the antagonism going on amongst the team centered around him. We also hadn't done our normal due diligence when hiring him because we were so impressed with his experience. It turns out he'd worked for more than a dozen organizations in the last 20 years.

A few months later, we ended up hiring a perfect replacement. She was everything we'd been looking for and is completely aligned and committed to our company. We've never looked back."

Stories like this are not uncommon. A lot of people don't know how to comfortably and confidently take action when faced with team members who aren't working out. What we do know is what we want our ideal team members to look like: We want to work with people who are intelligent, collaborative, creative, committed to producing top-quality work, and aligned with our values and with accomplishing our company's goals.

However, the reality is sometimes different. Team members may not have the necessary experience, their value system may not align with yours, and they may be putting their own goals ahead of the company's. All of these situations have the potential to restrict growth and even cause harm.

This is why it's crucial to pay close attention to anyone who may be having a negative impact on your overall organization. Be vigilant about the quality of team members you work with, and practice multiplication by subtraction when necessary.

TAKEAWAYS

The core of your business is all about autonomy—being in charge of your bigger future. In the words of Dan Sullivan, "If you don't take charge of your future, others will." Don't be afraid of saying goodbye to wrong-fit team members—design the team you want.

Chapter 3
Why Don't We Deal With Wrong-Fit Team Members?

Now that we've talked about the importance of having right-fit team members and the impacts of having wrong-fit people on your team, let's look at why it can be so difficult to make the hard decisions.

From my experience, the realization that a team member is no longer a right fit is much more complex than we realize. There are a lot of obstacles that make it a very challenging situation to deal with. It's also a confrontation that most people would *much* rather avoid.

As a leader in an organization, though, it's essential that you feel confident taking action in this area when necessary.

It takes commitment and courage to make the hard decisions. Remember, people look to you for direction, and your actions—and non-actions—speak volumes. Getting started is as simple as shifting your mindset. By bringing subtle clues to the fore-front, paying attention, and realizing the cost of continuing to employ a wrong-fit person, you're less likely to procrastinate about letting someone go.

Here are some of the reasons we hesitate and delay ending relationships with team members:

- ⊗ **We dread confrontation.** We avoid making a decision because we're afraid of dealing with people's reactions.
- ⊗ **Tears.** Most of us *really* don't like tears. Although they're rare, sometimes they're unavoidable.
- ⊗ **We think it's our fault.** We think we should have done more to help that person be successful.
- ⊗ **Loyalty.** This team member has been with us for a long time or during tough times. They're a good person and we don't want them to get hurt. We feel responsible for them.
- ⊗ **We don't see the issue clearly.** Often, when someone isn't a right fit for your company, they're good at hiding out. They're good at looking capable to you while having a negative impact on the rest of the team.
- ⊗ **We're afraid of legal ramifications.** We worry that if we don't execute the process properly, we could be sued.
- ⊗ **We think we need the "warm body."** We don't think we have the time to look for a new person to fill the role, so we live with an imperfect situation just to have someone there.
- ⊗ **We fear the work will come back to us.** We worry that in letting someone go, we'll be stuck with an even bigger workload.
- ⊗ **We think team morale might take a hit.** Will the rest of the team be worried that they'll be next?
- ⊗ **We can't pinpoint the problem.** We have a vague sense that something is wrong, but we're not sure exactly what it is and don't have hard evidence, so we don't take action.
- ⊗ **Hiring is hard.** Even if someone is hard to work with, we feel it will be harder to find someone else.
- ⊗ **They still get great results.** Despite their bad behavior, they're productive and bringing in revenue.

These are all examples of justifications that lead us directly to inaction. We procrastinate, we delay, and we distract ourselves with more urgent issues to postpone dealing with these very detrimental situations. The reality is that if you're having any of these thoughts, it's a clue that there's a problem on your team that needs your attention.

I've been there; I know what this feels like. I remember blaming myself for the slow progress of a new hire. I thought I hadn't done enough and that I needed to offer more direction. It's taken me years to realize that sometimes people are just the wrong fit. Great team members are great from the get-go. You can't hold yourself responsible for those who aren't stepping up to the plate.

There's a huge cost involved when we keep wrong-fit team members on board and let the problem fester.

Not only does it have a negative impact on you and your team, it impacts the person who's struggling as well. If someone's not a right fit, they're likely aware that they're not succeeding and will become resigned. The longer you ignore the problem, the more entrenched and stuck they become.

If you're noticing something's not working, at some level it's not healthy for them either. The role is not making the best use of them or their talents. Letting them go will actually be an opportunity for them to grow.

As leaders, it's our job to address the situation head-on. Otherwise, we're sending the message that this behavior is okay. As a result, the person has less incentive to change and more incentive to maintain the status quo.

Dan Sullivan rightly points out that, "Our problem is that we want to avoid suffering in life, and that isn't always possible. But you do have a choice—do you want short suffering or long suffering?"

The quicker you address team members who are no longer a right fit, the quicker you'll be able to move forward and avoid long-term suffering. And in the words of Dr. Henry Cloud, "You get what you tolerate." Wrong-fit team members, just like the lowest common denominator, lower the standards and weaken right-fit team members' overall engagement and commitment to your company.

For the benefit of your company's well being, stop justifying the behavior of team members who are clearly not a right fit. If you know it's the right time, find the courage to take the required next step to upgrade your team.

TAKEAWAYS

"Your biggest procrastinations are always telling you the most important things to work on next."

Dan Sullivan

Chapter 4
The Cost Of Not Taking Action

I want you to think about multiplication by subtraction as a strategy for growth. It's a necessary part of entrepreneurial life. I've experienced the transformational power that letting go of a team member can have on the health of a company.

We had a long-time team member who, from a results perspective, was very good at her job. However, over time, we slowly began to realize how toxic her attitude was. She was completely disingenuous and wasn't trusted by anyone on the team. Her presence was tearing down morale and damaging our company culture.

The final straw came with the implementation of a new system. She was totally resistant. Not only was she uninterested in learning it, she was negative and disrespectful during training. She also refused to accept the help volunteered by her peers. This behavior validated what we'd all been thinking, so, finally, we let her go.

A few months later, when meeting with a colleague, we were discussing things we were excited about. The first thing on her list was the dismissal of this particular team member. Given that my colleague is always positive and supportive, this was a bit shocking and unexpected. She explained how much this person's negativity had impacted everyone in the office. She didn't even think this person would be missed in terms of results. Negative people bring down really good people and keep them from reaching their full potential. This is why subtraction can make such a difference.

Take a look at some of the costs that can result from not dealing with wrong-fit team members:

- **Dollar cost.** It's very expensive to keep someone on the team who shouldn't be there, especially long term. Because they're not committed to bringing in results and detract from other people's ability to do their jobs well, it impacts revenue, profit, and the bottom line.
- **Toxic to the team and company culture.** Wrong-fit team members can be distracting, disruptive, and hard to work with. People end up having to work around them and clean up their messes, lowering their productivity.
- **Creates friction and drag.** They slow down projects and teamwork.
- **Causes you to lose good people.** If you neglect taking action, other team members will naturally question your leadership and why you seem to be satisfied with substandard performance.
- **Occupies your energy and time.** Problematic team members take up your time and mental energy—energy that could be used for much more strategic business thinking.
- **Time-consuming for management.** Managers constantly have to be alert, checking up, and ready to handle any issues that arise with wrong-fit team members.

- **Negatively impacts the team member.** Not being a right-fit team member is hard, and the longer the behavior continues, the more ingrained their negative attitudes and behaviors become.
- **Damaging to your company's reputation.** Keeping these team members on board could result in a loss of credibility and the referability of your company.
- **Demoralizing to their team.** Wrong-fit team leaders leave their team feeling like nothing is ever right or good enough, keeping the team stagnant and unable to capitalize on new opportunities, creativity, and growth.

Multiplication by subtraction is a way to make sure your organization is always thriving and growing. Gardeners often prune dead or dying sections off plants to allow the healthier parts to thrive rather than struggling to support the dead weight. When you decide to "let go to grow," you'll find that everyone is relieved and had wondered why you didn't take action sooner. You'll realize that not only were the results the wrong-fit team members were producing exaggerated, but that your team is more creative without them. This is the multiplication experienced through multiplication by subtraction.

If we hang onto relationships that are just okay, we're siding with complacency. It's only by pruning relationships that we can achieve the success we're really striving for.

TAKEAWAYS
Negative people bring down really good people and keep them from reaching their full potential.

Part 2 Powerful Tools For Diagnosing And Strategizing When It Comes To Subtraction

Chapter 5
Symptoms, Clues, And What To Look For

How do you know you have a problem?

And at what point should you let someone go?

It's easy to be decisive if a team member does something discernably wrong, like steal from you or harm someone.

However, most problematic behaviors are more subtle. People are complex and we're busy. It can be easy to miss signs that things aren't working.

When behaviors are less apparent, they're harder to deal with. This is why properly addressing these issues as soon as they come to light makes a huge difference in the long run.

Have a look at the following chart, which brings awareness to the many different ways wrong-fit team members manifest themselves.

Are any of your team members displaying one or more of these symptoms? And can you afford to suffer the result and cost this is having on the rest of your team?

The symptoms on this list are clear indicators that a course correction needs to be made.

Symptom	Result & Cost

Malaise/Disengaged
They're not excited by their work, where the company's going, or anything else. They just show up. They don't put much effort or creativity into what they do and produce only enough to get by.

Mediocrity
The rest of the team feels like this person is dragging them down, and will start to bypass them.

Oppositional
They're always argumentative and tend to disagree with new innovations and improvements.

Friction
This can lead to a polarization within the team, slowing down or preventing new improvements from being implemented. The result is a loss in efficiency, morale, productivity, and profit.

They Can't Keep Pace
Their ability to learn is just not fast enough for them to keep up, and they slow everyone else down. They don't have the mental horsepower, skills, experience, or intelligence to properly perform in your environment.

Drag
This can really slow down the team because this person eventually becomes a roadblock to getting things done in a timely manner. They may feel bad but are simply unable to mentally speed up.

Drama Queen Or King
This person creates an enormous amount of unnecessary conflict and emotion around small issues and takes everything personally, taking everyone off task.

Distraction And Loss Of Focus
Drama is very distracting, wasting the time and mental and emotional energy of everyone involved. It also diverts people's focus to non-essential issues.

Not Accountable
This person doesn't deliver the goods. They're also an expert at covering their tracks and diverting attention from themselves.

Loss Of Momentum
When counted on to deliver key information and results, they'll always have an excuse for why it's not done. These team members take up a disproportionate amount of everyone's time because people end up covering for them.

Focused On Status
They'll do what they need to do to get ahead so they can forward their own career—often at the company's expense.

Politics And Silos
Instead of working as part of a team, they'll put their energy toward building their own power base and reputation. This is energy that needs to be focused on growing the company, not advancing their place in the pecking order.

Symptom

Result & Cost

Entitlement Attitude
This person feels they're entitled to rights and privileges. They're takers, not givers. They're more focused on their rights than their responsibilities. Often, they're a top performer and feel as though they're owed more than what they're getting.

Resistance
They're often hard to satisfy and won't "take one for the team." You'll spend time bargaining with them to get things done because they don't care to contribute unless they know it will be recognized.

Clueless
This person exhibits a lack of awareness about themselves, how they come across, and the value of their contribution. Attempts to enlighten them are met with a lack of comprehension.

Roadblock
It takes an enormous amount of time to work with this person because it takes them a long time to grasp certain concepts. It's very challenging to help them make changes in behavior so they can be more effective.

Uncooperative And Non-Collaborative
They're tough to work with and not open to other people's input or suggestions.

Stalemate
Projects get stuck and decisions don't get made because they insist on doing things their way. Going against them requires outside intervention or is a guaranteed power struggle.

Lack Of Integrity
They feel the end justifies the means and there is no need to honor their word or live up to expectations. Often, they also assume other people don't have integrity or are out to get them, and act accordingly.

Lack Of Trust And Teamwork
Trust is the basis of effective teamwork. When someone can't be counted on to look out for others or do the right thing, it taints the whole team.

Arrogance (aka "God's gift to your company")
People who think they're the smartest and most valuable member on the team don't leave room for contribution from others. They think others are less important. Consequently, they don't listen, and they treat people like objects instead of valued team members.

Disempowerment
When one person thinks they have all the answers, they don't recognize the value of other people's input, disempowering everyone else. The rest of the team doesn't feel valued and may stop contributing.

Not Adaptable
Your organization is changing but this person is not changing with it. They're a relic of your legacy, and the team is increasingly having to work around them.

Resentment
As your right-fit team aligns around your bigger future, this person increasingly stands out as a burden that everyone else must carry.

How many of these warning signs resonated with you? Did any team members' names, current or past, come to mind?

Ideally, a conversation will be enough to address what's currently not working. Some people will be open to being coached out of unproductive attitudes and mindsets. But if they're not, you need to accept that it will slowly infect your entire team if they're kept on board. In one way or another, you need to take action. And it may be time to consider making a "necessary ending."

A word to the wise — align on values. Your success depends on making sure that your team members' values are aligned with yours.

Our values affect the way we behave and how we think, and they're the basis for every decision we make. This is why it's so important to make sure your team supports you in this way. It makes teamwork more straightforward because people understand one another and do the right things for the right reasons.

When you have a clearly defined set of guiding principles your team can refer to, it sets the tone for a healthy company culture and team members can better internalize what the organization cares about as a whole.

One of the biggest causes of misalignment in companies is that principles are not clearly articulated. For example, what takes precedence, timeliness or high-quality work? What actions and behaviors are rewarded, and what will you not put up with? These are things your team needs to know.

Keeping a team member on board whose values conflict with the company's can pull things off track and send the message that you're okay with the dissent and lack of similar core values.

The best companies develop an inside-out approach in order to make sure their team members are playing to the beat of the same drum.

Zappos, an online shoe and clothing company based out of Las Vegas, Nevada, is famous for their compelling set of values. It's become their mandate and a large part of how they define themselves as a brand:

As we grow as a company, it has become more and more important to explicitly define the core values from which we develop our culture, our brand, and our business strategies.

These are the ten core values that we live by:
1. *Deliver WOW Through Service*
2. *Embrace and Drive Change*
3. *Create Fun and A Little Weirdness*
4. *Be Adventurous, Creative, and Open-Minded*
5. *Pursue Growth and Learning*
6. *Build Open and Honest Relationships With Communication*
7. *Build a Positive Team and Family Spirit*
8. *Do More With Less*
9. *Be Passionate and Determined*
10. *Be Humble*

Zappos Family Core Values can be found at *zappos.com/core-values*

By publishing their mission statement and core values as a public document, they're establishing a relationship with future employees right away.

They're setting the tone and standard for who they want on their team. This is an incredibly smart way of ensuring their entire company is aligned in working toward common goals that support who they are and who they want to be in the future.

Creating a similar document for your company can be the answer to ensuring your team is always engaged and making the decisions that support your organization's future.

Use your values as a tool for attracting and keeping right-fit team members. Making them available through a tangible document can aid in communicating why someone may not be suitable for your company.

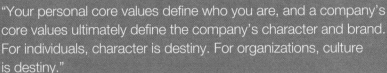

TAKEAWAYS

"Your personal core values define who you are, and a company's core values ultimately define the company's character and brand. For individuals, character is destiny. For organizations, culture is destiny."

Tony Hsieh, *Delivering Happiness: A Path to Profits, Passion, and Purpose.*

Chapter 6
Common Scenarios And Strategies

So now for the really tough question: What do you do if someone isn't acting like a right-fit team member? Multiplication by subtraction isn't always the immediate solution, although it might be necessary after you try other strategies first.

To help you gain confidence about reaching the best solution, here's a set of steps you can follow to create the best result for everyone.

Step 1 Identify

Figure out what type of issue you're dealing with, and identify any obstacles that may be standing in the way.

Step 2 Strategize

Strategize and take corrective action. Come up with a viable solution and try it out. If that doesn't work, try another. We believe in giving lots of chances, but we're also clear on where the boundaries lie. You may turn the team member around by shifting their responsibilities or by addressing their behavior and helping shift their mindset.

Step 3 Take Action

If nothing works, let go. If you've tried everything and are convinced that this is not a right-fit team member, strategize the best way to exit the person as gracefully as possible.

Let's run through some common scenarios and examples where someone's not showing up as a right-fit team member and what to do about it.

 Not as advertised.

This occurs either when you're hiring someone or moving an existing team member into a new role. These people look great on paper and interview well but may not be as capable as they first came across. This can be frustrating because, although you may have taken all the right steps, it's just not working out.

Reason we don't take action: We're not confident that we've trained them well enough. We assume it's our fault they're not performing up to standards.

What to do? Take the initiative and have a conversation outlining the issues. Clearly state your expectations and give them a reasonable time frame in which to improve. If they don't improve to meet your standards, you can be confident there's nothing more you can do. It's in your best interest to let them go.

Level of difficulty:

Example: *Jessa's interviews were fabulous. She was confident and poised, and had all the right experience. I was sure she'd be a powerful addition to the team and provide me with great leverage and support as my executive assistant.*

Unfortunately, this wasn't how it turned out. What she demon-strated in the interview was not what she brought to work. It took her three weeks to master simple, routine tasks that normally would have taken only a few days. What she thought was important didn't align with the priorities of the business. She spent an inordinate amount of time socializing and wasting other people's time—even the team had become unbelievably frustrated with her.

Fortunately, we took action within the three-month probation-ary period and decided to let her go. This was still a tough decision. It was really hard for me to come to terms with the fact that there was nothing else we could do. I really wanted it to work, and it wasn't until I had a long and thorough conversa-tion with our human resources director that I realized this was the best course of action. This isn't to say I didn't dread the conversation, but I knew it was the right thing to do.

 Right person, wrong role.

There are wonderful people who have great capabilities but they simply don't fit with their current role. At Strategic Coach, we've been very successful at moving these people into an-other position that's better suited to their talents. The Kolbe A™ Index has been an extremely useful tool in this situation. It measures how people strive and solve problems, offering insights into where they'll perform best.

The Kolbe Index can, for example, help you confidently move

someone from an administrative role where they're struggling into a sales role where they'll strive, based on their talent profile.

Reason we don't take action: We like them, they're a good person, and we believe they have potential. But without a strategic tool like The Kolbe System™, we don't know what to do and feel bad about letting them go.

What to do? If the person's attitude and aptitude are there— and their job isn't a right fit look for another role for them in your company, one where they'll blossom. If not, then it's a graceful exit.

Level of difficulty:

Example: *In 1990, Paulette was hired to be the receptionist at Strategic Coach. Two of her sisters were already working with us, so we were pleased to have her on the team. Her responsibilities spanned many areas, including scheduling, bookkeeping, and workshop setups. We were still such a new company, it was all hands on deck. But it was apparent she was struggling in her role. She was often frustrated, making it difficult to work with her. We recognized she hadn't quite found her spot in the company, but we knew her heart was in it, so we kept encouraging her to try out new things. Susan, one of our sales associates and Paulette's older sister, was going on vacation for a couple of weeks. Before she left, she approached Paulette and told her to get on the phone while she was away to see if she could sign anyone up for the Program. And that was it! It* *was the answer Paulette had been searching for—connecting with prospects fed her soul. In 1995, she made the leap into an official sales role, and today, she's still highly motivated. She's grown into a real superstar in the company as one of our primary event speakers, an international sales specialist, and a highly engaged team member.*

 The warm body who has stopped growing, aka "the zombie."

These people come on board and jump into their role full of energy, showing great initiative and talent. However, they eventually plateau and are only committed to staying within their comfort zone. They're really just there. It's difficult to let them go because you know what they're capable of when they're motivated and engaged.

Reason we don't take action: We don't want to let go of someone who we know has the skills and talent to excel in their role. This is one of the most challenging situations to handle, because these team members have the capabilities but have become completely stagnant in their professional growth. However, because of their unwillingness to succeed and take on new responsibilities and challenges, at a basic level, they create friction and drag. Even though it can be quite a tough decision, if you take action graciously, people will respect your judgment.

What to do? Really evaluate the cost of keeping this person on the team. If you're growing and they're not, they're holding you back. Ask them whether they're willing to rise up and grow. If they're not, determine an appropriate exit package, and your relationship will most likely survive.

Level of difficulty:

Example: *We had a team member, Anton, who was very productive and capable in his administrative role. It was a tough position to fill—supporting two busy, innovative, unstructured entrepreneurs. However, it became evident over time that he'd fallen into a rut. He refused to take on new opportunities outside the narrow bounds of his role and didn't see a problem with this. He also developed an entitlement attitude and refused to put in any more effort than necessary. Working around him became more trouble than it was worth. Eventually, because he wasn't growing along with the company, he was let go. It was a shock to him, but afterward his friends let us know that he had some awareness of what went wrong and regretted having taken the role for granted.*

High performers — with really bad habits and poor teamwork skills.

This situation is not as straightforward as the others. These team members have really poor teamwork habits like not showing up on time, a lack of communication skills, and accountability or behavioral issues. However, they may also be top performers bringing in half of the region's sales. This becomes very problematic because they're aware of the value they're creating and are confident you won't fire them. In a sense, they'll hold you hostage if you let them.

Reason we don't take action: It can feel very expensive to let this person go, and it may feel like your bottom line will suffer without them.

What to do? Since they're valuable in terms of results, it's worthwhile to do some intense coaching with them. If the problem is a lack of self-awareness or personality traits they're not managing well, they may be able to improve on them. Be very clear about your expectations, and if you set consequences for poor habits, attitude, and behavior, you need to be prepared to follow through. Most important, this person needs to acknowledge that they're doing something wrong. They also need to make it clear that they're open and willing to making improvements in these areas.

You also need to be extremely aware of the message this may be sending to others. Do you value behavior and teamwork, or are your results the only priority? If your company culture is driven by teamwork, then behavior that contradicts that must have a consequence. You may be forced to make a tough decision. What's more important—staying true to your company's values or your bottom line results?

If the person isn't willing or able to change, you'll need to let them go. You both need to accept that, although you tried, it's not a workable situation.

Level of difficulty: ⬤ ⬤ ⬤ ⬤ ⬤

Example: *Our company culture thrives on entrepreneurial energy. This became very apparent when we brought in experienced senior managers to run our various teams. Clara was one of these new hires. She was very skilled and book smart, but we quickly realized she lacked essential teamwork skills. She only paid lip service to collaborating, didn't take into account other people's input, preferred to work in isolation, and always thought her way was best. She was highly resistant to feedback and advice. Overall, the team felt she was very patronizing. Team members later admitted they even considered quitting because of how difficult it became to work with her. I stepped in to offer personal coaching, but this was met with anger and resentment. Two weeks later, she resigned, which solved the problem for us.*

 High performers — with the wrong value system.

This type of situation is often found in senior leadership positions. These particular team members are ambitious, capable, and appreciated for the value they create for the company. The problem is that they're doing it for status, not contribution. They're building a power base, polarizing others, and protecting their turf. This type of person may actually be the most detrimental to your organization, especially in terms of team development.

If your goal is to surround yourself with a right-fit team that works creatively and collaboratively, these people have a major impact on whether this is possible. They're interested only in their own success, not the company's. At some point, they're going to want more than is available to them.

Ultimately, they're there for their reasons, at the expense of yours. Alignment isn't always possible with these people, and when values diverge, it's time to say goodbye.

Reason we don't take action: These are the hardest people to let go because they're often the ones most deeply embedded within your organization. They have a high level of responsibility and leverage you by taking tasks and projects off your plate that you no longer have time for.

What to do? Be extremely cautious in this situation. Ultimately, if they prioritize their goals over yours, they'll end up making decisions to benefit themselves and not the organization. You don't want to be the one who pays the price for that, or your company will be the one losing out. The sooner you get them off the team, the healthier your organization will be.

Letting these people go may take some finesse, because reputation and appearances are so important to them. The most strategic approach to letting them go is to address it as a parting of ways. If they're a partner, you may need to buy them out. If they're a long-standing team member, consider whether a generous severance package is a possibility. In the long term, it will cost you less, reduce stress, and give you more peace of mind.

You also need to trust that you and your team will be fine. Keep your eye out for great talent. Quite often, there are capable people internally who may not have been able to grow under that person's leadership. Ask your team for recommendations and tap into your network for new talent.

Level of difficulty:

Example: *I was in the process of replacing myself as president and CEO of my company. Doug came into the picture at just the right time. He had decades of experience in his industry and shared a very similar vision for the future of the company. I was thrilled to start the transition of moving Doug into the role of CEO. It would relieve me of day-to-day management and free me up to do what I did best—be the founder and Chief Visionary.*

Things started off on a bad note right away. Doug refused to take the position unless his title was announced and made known from the outset—he wanted the fancy title. I was reluctant to do this until I felt Doug had earned it, but against my instincts, I went along with the request and made the announcement to the company and clients with great fanfare.

Unfortunately, only seven months later, Doug had to be let go. Results hadn't improved at all since bringing him on board; they were actually worse than before he started. The final straw came when I found out that Doug was actively promoting himself—and not the company—to clients, and building up his own reputation at the expense of the company.

There were several clues to Doug's lack of alignment before-

hand, some of which had to do with differences between Doug's and my value systems. In addition, we also had very different personalities and opposite Kolbe profiles. I was a man of action, whereas Doug focused on creating a "living document" of key plans and initiatives. The problem was that Doug's focus was on the document, not on producing actual results. Ultimately, Doug and I were unable to align on our values and priorities.

High-level people have a big impact on companies, and it's important to realize their reach. As Patrick Lencioni examines in his insightful book *The Advantage*, it's when we allow for misalignment at the top levels of our companies that we leave room for dysfunction with the team.

 Scenario 5 **Legacy team members.**

These people have been with us for a long time. They're often the ones who've been there since the beginning, helped us get started, and stuck with us through thick and thin. We appreciate their loyalty, and not only are we fond of them, we feel a sense of responsibility for them.

Unfortunately, though, they sometimes plateau and stop growing. They may not fit in with how the company is developing or are unable to keep up with the pace of change. They often pine for "the good old days" when they were closer to the decision makers and when less was required of them. They resist new systems and aren't able to provide new value. We end up working around them to get things done.

Reason we don't take action: Again, we feel guilty about letting someone go who's been so dedicated. We often know their families and feel a certain responsibility for their financial well being (especially if we're not confident in their ability to find a similar job). They're good people who deserve to be treated well, and we don't know what to do, so we avoid the issue.

What to do? It's vital to have ongoing conversations with them about their lack of growth and contribution. They're usually aware that things aren't working but may not know how to make the change themselves. Talk through their options. Let them know what opportunities there are, both internally and outside the company. When it's clear that their future is elsewhere, give them a time frame of three months, for example, to find another opportunity, and help them in any way you can. Reach out to your network, provide reference letters, and give them time for interviews. Once the agreed-upon time limit has passed, follow through and say goodbye.

Level of difficulty: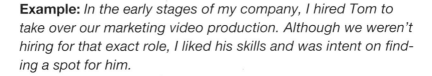

Example: *In the early stages of my company, I hired Tom to take over our marketing video production. Although we weren't hiring for that exact role, I liked his skills and was intent on finding a spot for him.*

The struggles started from the get-go. Tom was excellent at getting great footage, but when it came to creating content, he was the ultimate perfectionist. I needed short video content fast. Our marketing didn't require full-length documentary-style footage, but this went against everything he wanted to do and felt was important.

Tom's strengths and talents were not a right-fit for his role. I was aware of this, but instead of accepting it and letting him go, we struggled along, moving him into various roles, including Director of Marketing. He was capable in these different positions but was hard to work with. He wanted things to go back to how they'd been when the company was smaller. I spent over ten years trying to fix a situation that couldn't be fixed.

Eventually, the tension and stress became too much. This one person pushing back all the time began to break the entire team. After a very honest conversation, Tom admitted that with the way things were going, it just wasn't going to work anymore.

I knew a change was in order, but it was hard because I only wanted the best for him, and I knew he was a good man. People felt loyal to him. He was part of the company when it started to bloom. We knew his family, and we knew that he was struggling to find himself. We agreed he would take three months to find a new job. I didn't tell anyone and didn't start scouting out new employees. I also offered to look at his résumé, write letters of recommendation, and connect him with people in my network, none of which he took me up on.

Three months had come and gone, and Tom hadn't found new work. But I knew the only reason I hadn't let him go was *because I really wanted to help him.*

But you can only help those who want to be helped, so I followed through and said goodbye to Tom. I knew I couldn't avoid the problem any longer—multiplication by subtraction was the next step.

What is most apparent about each of these situations is that when running any successful business, you will encounter and have to learn how to deal with team members who are no longer performing at the right speed and level for your organization.

Here are the three scenarios we hear most often when it comes to strategizing on the most gracious way to let someone go:

1. **Someone's abilities are no longer a right-fit for the company, and you're going to work with them to help them find a new opportunity for which they're better suited.** You provide reference letters, introductions, and time to go on interviews. This process often happens over a period of months and is very collaborative.

2. **You make the decision that someone needs to leave, but they've been with you a long time and you respect and appreciate their contribution.** In this case, they agree to resign, they send out the communication to the team, and they'll often work for a few days to finish off and transition their projects.

3. **You've made the decision that a team member needs to leave immediately, and it may be a risk to allow them to continue to access your confidential information.**
   This situation is the most challenging. In Part 3, I'll provide some guidelines for what we've found to be the most effective way of handling it.

Every situation will be different, but by adopting a mindset where you're paying attention and always ready to take action and address issues of this kind as soon as they cross your field of view, you'll avoid a lot of pain and distress.

TAKEAWAYS
Multiplication by subtraction isn't always the immediate solution.

Chapter 7
Tools For Proper Diagnosis

Knowing whether it's necessary to subtract in order to multiply won't always be obvious. Too often, we know there's a problem, but we don't know how to identify it. To guide you, we've outlined the most effective profiles and assessment tools we've found to help you diagnose the issue properly.

You can think of these tools as extremely useful lenses to assess whether a team member is a right fit for their role.

Where is the problem stemming from?

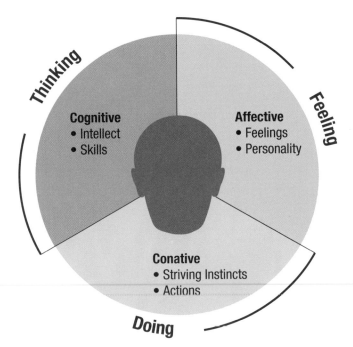

Thinking

Cognitive
- Intellect
- Skills

Affective
- Feelings
- Personality

Feeling

Conative
- Striving Instincts
- Actions

Doing

It's most useful to consider all parts of the mind:

Cognitive
Cognitive is the part of the mind dedicated to thinking. It includes learning, intelligence, skills, reason, education, and experience, and can be measured through IQ and other skill-testing instruments.

Affective
Affective refers to a person's personality preferences. This is the part of the mind that includes feelings, desires, emotions, values, and motivations. Personality analyses can be used to assess this part of the mind.

Conative
Conative is the *doing* part of the mind. It measures mental energy, a person's instinctive way of taking action—their striving instincts, which can be validated by completing a Kolbe A™ Index.

When we view our team members through these three lenses, we can choose the right tools to evaluate their capabilities in different areas. A personality concern, for instance, is very different from an issue relating to a lack of skills or experience. A conative mismatch for the role is also a very distinct type of issue. When we're clear on the type of problem we need to fix, it helps us take action and move forward with what to do, and avoid what not to do.

Let's have a quick look at what the three different types of assessments—each focused on a different part of the mind—can tell us.

1. Cognitive Assessments

Cognitive tools will help you to determine if the issue lies in a lack of skill, training, knowledge, experience, or intellect. Does this particular team member have the mental horsepower to do the job at the pace needed in your environment? Do they have the depth—and the breadth—required?

? Questions to ask right away:

- Does this person have the right training for their job?
- Can they learn quickly enough for what's required?
- Do they have the background and experience to respond to situations appropriately?
- Do they have the raw intelligence required for their role?
- Are they clear on the results they're responsible for delivering?
- Are they picking up and retaining the key information in a timely fashion?

If you answered "yes" to these questions, you're likely not dealing with an intellect issue. If you answered "no" to any of these questions, either you need to do additional training or you need to assess whether this person has the right mental bandwidth required for their position.

⚙ What tools or profiles can you use?

Use IQ tests or specific knowledge tests. At Strategic Coach, we use the Wonderlic test, which assesses intelligence and lists intellect scores required for different roles. It's proven extremely useful to determine the best candidates for hiring.

2. Affective (Personality) Assessments

Affective tools help determine how a person's personality will gel with their role and the workplace culture. There are many different dimensions to these types of analyses: how introverted or extroverted a person is, whether they approach tasks in a fast-paced or even-paced manner, or how focused they are. For example, some people prefer high-speed environments and are extremely outgoing, while others are more laid back and reserved. Some are more people-focused while others have a preference for focusing on tasks. These are all part of the affective world, and certain roles can require a particular personality type. However, the affective arena is also where the opportunities for personality conflicts lie.

Questions to ask right away:
- Does this person operate at the right pace for their role?
- Are other people on the team frustrated by the speed at which they work?
- Are they a people person or a task-focused person? Does this match what their role requires?
- Do you feel as though they care about your clients and customers?
- Is their priority getting things done or are they often found socializing around the office?
- Do they have the right set of strengths for the role?

If you suspect that someone's personality is the reason they may not be the right fit for your company, use one of the tools listed on the next page to confirm whether this is the issue.

Gaining a better understanding of someone's character may be enough to resolve the situation. It may require a slight realignment of your expectations, a deepening of their own self-awareness, or finding a better spot for them within your company that would benefit from their approach. This is not a bad thing. Expecting everyone to be exactly the same is very limiting when it comes to building an effective team.

What tools or profiles can you use?

Common personality profiles are:

- DISC Assessment
- Myers Briggs Type Indicator®
- Social Styles by Wilson Learning®
- Lumina Spark Personality Test
- Enneagram
- The Predictive Index
- Clifton StrengthsFinder®

Note: StrengthsFinder can be used only as a development tool. It is not meant to be utilized during the hiring process. At Strategic Coach, we use DISC in the hiring process and Strengths-Finder as soon as someone has started with the company.

3. Conative Assessment

Conation is likely the dimension you're least aware of, but it's one of the most important. I've seen it happen far too often that people are let go because of "personality conflicts" when it's really a mismatch in how they initiate action or what their role requires of them. The Kolbe Conative Index® designed by Kathy Kolbe explains that there is something other than personality and intelligence at work in the human mind. It provides invaluable insight into how people naturally do things, allowing you to maximize people's talents and mental energy. Because it measures striving instincts and mental energy, you can identify whether a team member may be experiencing strain because their role isn't allowing them to take action in the ways they naturally strive to get things done, or tension if their manager's expectations differ from how they naturally problem-solve.

Questions to ask right away:

- Are you asking them to perform a task substantially differently from their natural modes of problem-solving?
- Are they operating in ways completely opposite to you?
- Do they seem to run out of mental energy and burn out easily?
- Do they take a significantly longer time to complete tasks than others?
- Are they exhausted and drained by the end of the workday?
- Are other team members frustrated because this person doesn't do things the way they expect?

If you answered "yes" to any of these questions, it's an indication that this person is struggling because they're being asked to perform in a way that is not at all innate to them. Introducing an awareness of conation into your workplace, and giving people the freedom to be who they are, can have dramatic effects on your business.

What tools or profiles can you use?

Kolbe Corp offers a wide array of indices, products, and services that can benefit training and growth in your business. Not only do we have all Strategic Coach clients do the Kolbe A™ Index, we have all potential new hires do it as well.

Profiles, hiring, and liability concerns.

When using psychometric profiles for hiring, it's critical that you educate yourself on how to use them responsibly from a legal standpoint. Profiles must be used consistently with each candidate you're considering for the role. You can't pick and choose whom to profile; it has to be the same process for each applicant.

Using profiles with candidates has another great benefit. It prevents you from hiring great interviewees who turn out to be subpar once in their role. People may nail the interview process and be superb at presenting one facet of themselves but show up entirely differently when hired. Profiles are the key to gaining great insight and clarity into the many different aspects of an individual.

TAKEAWAYS

"An organization's greatest competitive advantage lies in building employee teams that have a synergistic mix of Striving Instincts. Teams composed of the right combination of MOs will unleash an energy that goes beyond that of a mere collection of individuals."

Kathy Kolbe, *Pure Instinct: The M.O. of High Performance People and Teams*

Multiplication By Subtraction

Part 3 **How To Take Action With Confidence**

Chapter 8
How To Let Go To Grow

My hope is that by sharing my experience, advice, strategies, and stories, I've helped you appreciate that multiplication by subtraction is both important and natural to the growth process.

If I can take you back to *Necessary Endings*, Cloud uses the brilliant analogy of gardening to illustrate why "growth depends on getting rid of the unwanted or the superfluous."

"Pruning," he says, "is a process of proactive endings. It turns out that a rose bush, like many other plants, cannot reach its full potential without a very systematic process of pruning. The gardener intentionally and purposefully cuts off branches and buds that fall into any of three categories:

1. Healthy buds or branches that are not the best ones,
2. Sick branches that are not going to get well, and
3. Dead branches that are taking up space needed for the healthy ones to thrive."

He goes on, "The areas of your business and life that require your limited resources—your time, energy, talent, emotions, money—but are not achieving the vision you have for them should be pruned."

Think of your company as a living organism. Breakdowns need to happen for growth. Sometimes, you need a breakdown to inspire a breakthrough.

Physical exercise, for example, stimulates organic growth in your body. You're building new muscles and rejuvenating your lungs as you challenge them against resistance.

This type of organic growth should also exist within your company, especially when it comes to your team. Just like our bodies and plants need to shed certain things to keep growing, so too do our companies. It's helpful to no one if we falsify things by saying that everyone we've ever hired is still the right person to be on the team.

An ending can be the decision that alleviates unhappiness and alters our path for the better. It also invites the question of how committed you are to reaching your full potential, because the reality is that you can't get where you're going if you have team members who are weighing you down. And remember, if it's not working for you, it's likely not working for them at some level too.

So if you're committed to being at the top of your game, and you're ready to let go of the relationships that are no longer contributing to your purpose—these are important things to keep in mind.

More important than anything else is the health of your overall company. If you know someone is no longer a right fit, trust your gut on this. It's normal to have feelings of guilt, disbelief, fear, and uncertainty and to want to avoid the issue altogether.

But this shouldn't be a justification for not taking action. Think of the cost of having a wrong-fit player on your team and how much this pulls everyone down.

Focusing on your vision and consciously changing your mindset will provide you with the confidence you need to take action. It's also about getting very clear about the truth of the situation: "I wish this had worked, but it didn't. Now, I'm going to find the best way to deal with it."

Action is almost always better than no action. The health of your team makes a huge difference to the momentum of your business. So adopt a productive and courageous mindset because everyone, including you, has a stake in upholding the standards of the business.

The decision to let someone go can be an emotionally taxing one. But it's been my experience that the healthiest way to think about it is that you're *responsible to* your team members, but you're not *responsible for* them.

Are you responsible for letting someone go gracefully and with dignity? Absolutely.

But are you responsible for their overall success and what they decide to do with the rest of their life? No.

Being fired is usually a massive reality check for people, and it can certainly be a blow to their ego—but this doesn't mean it's something they can't recover and learn from. I've had people tell me that being fired was one of the best things to ever happen to them. It ended up being a chance for them to get grounded in what they really wanted to be doing and to find an even better way to contribute their talents to the world. It can be a harsh, abrupt transition, but it can also be incredibly healthy. If it's seen as a learning experience, it can be a very humbling, transformative event for people.

Freeing people up to go back into the marketplace is beneficial for your company but also for them. You're putting them in a position where they can create value and ideally do something that's more meaningful to them.

Leadership is doing the right thing. As a leader, you're in charge of growing people and managing talent and resources. This is why it's your responsibility to have the tough conversations when someone is no longer compatible with your company. It's about always having the bigger picture and greater good in mind.

Make it a habit to continuously ask yourself who's a right fit, who's not, what type of talent you're trying to attract, and how you can keep your best team members.

Focus your mindset on building the longevity of your company. You want your business to live far past you, so this means digging in when things get challenging—we're all guilty of keeping someone on the team for too long.

Look at your team from all different angles and determine whether someone is holding you back. If they are, there's often a considerate and respectful way to approach and solve the situation.

So, how do you actually go about letting someone go? Each situation is different, but we believe in due diligence and making the transition as smooth as possible. When dealing with termination, treat every circumstance as its own special case. Of the utmost importance is treating people with respect, gratitude, and empathy. Here are some guidelines for structuring your version of a graceful exit.

Before: Get Prepared

- **Get expert advice and consult an employment lawyer.** Be sure you understand what you can and can't offer a departing team member since countries, states, and provinces have different employment laws.

- **Prepare the paperwork.** Have any documents that need to be signed or taken care of ready.

- **Take security precautions.** Be prepared to change passwords and codes, and restrict access to databases, email, etc.

- **Make a plan for how the person's work is going to be handled.** Figure out who's going to take over key responsibilities and for how long. If you're replacing the person, get ready to start the hiring process.

During: The Conversation

- **Having the conversation.** This is the part the majority of leaders dread the most. When it comes down to actually having the conversation, people often expect that the confrontation will be a lot worse than it actually turns out to be.

- **Where?** Choose somewhere private. You want to be sure it's somewhere you can both speak plainly, and privacy is of utmost importance.

- **Be brief.** Be sure to communicate the purpose of the meeting in the first 30 seconds. The best coaching I've received is to keep it short, factual, and to the point. Say something along the lines of, "I've made a decision, and unfortunately, today is your last day." Concisely explain your reasons, such as, "We don't find that you're a right fit for this role." You may need to provide specific examples, but be clear that the decision is final and non-negotiable. The total meeting time will often be 15 minutes or less.

- **Go through the specifics.** Explain the details of what happens next. For example, they will clear out their desk, hand over keys and passwords, and so on. Explain any paperwork you're giving them.

- **Pack up.** If they're leaving that day, escort them to their office space so they can pack up their personal effects, or make arrangements to ship them at a later date.

- **Get them home safe.** Make sure they're okay to drive, or if they don't drive, arrange for transportation so they get home safely.

After: Tying Up Loose Ends

- **Communicate.** Send an email to your team notifying them of the change and that you wish the person well. Let your team know who they can talk with if they have questions.

- **Reassure.** If the person's firing will be unexpected for your team, they may need to be reassured that their jobs are secure and that they don't need to worry.

- **Distribute the work.** Divide up the person's responsibilities to the remaining team members so that nothing falls through the cracks. If you haven't already, start the hiring process for the person's replacement.

The best-case scenario is the team member will have anticipated it and understand why the decision was made. They may even let you know how much they enjoyed working for you and how much they appreciated everybody on the team. In this case, they might also want to give you the status on all their current projects so things can be easily handed off. This isn't the most common reaction, but these people truly do want to leave things on the best note possible.

There's also the likelihood that someone could have a negative reaction and be completely shocked and blindsided by the news. If this is the case, the best thing you can do is listen and offer your compassion, but be clear that you're holding firm on your decision. You don't want someone to leave feeling angry or upset, but you can only be responsible for your part of the interaction. Do what you can to part on good terms.

Regardless of why someone isn't working out in your company, you still want them to land successfully on their feet. If you can support them to do that in any way, all the better. Ideally, their departure will lead them to a place where they can make better use of their unique talents and skills.

I encourage you to always be honest with yourself and embrace the benefits of upholding the highest standards for your team. Practicing multiplication by subtraction can change the path of your business.

Don't second guess, have confidence, and give yourself permission to take action.

TAKEAWAYS

Letting go of wrong-fit people with negative attitudes sends out a powerful, positive message to everyone else: You're committed to having a quality team and a quality organization. By curating your team, you'll continue to attract and retain great talent.

Appendix

About Strategic Coach®

The Strategic Coach® Program, founded in 1989 by Dan Sullivan and Babs Smith, was the first coaching program exclusively for entrepreneurs. It remains the most innovative in terms of its ability to help participants make successive quantum leaps toward increasingly greater personal and professional goals.

Strategic Coach clients today not only significantly increase their income and free time, they build strong, future-focused companies that leave their competition behind. Many have set new standards in their industries and made significant contributions to their communities through the increased focus, resources, and creativity gained by participating in the Program.

The Strategic Coach Inc.
Strategic Coach is an organization created by entrepreneurs, for entrepreneurs, and operates using the same philosophy, tools, and concepts taught in The Strategic Coach Program. With over 100 entrepreneurially-minded team members and four offices—Toronto, Chicago, Los Angeles, and the UK— the company continues to grow and enrich its offerings to an expanding global client base. Currently, over 3,000 successful and highly motivated entrepreneurs from over 60 industries and a dozen countries attend Strategic Coach workshops on a quarterly basis.

If you'd like more information about Strategic Coach, its programs for entrepreneurs at all levels of success, or its many products for entrepreneurial thinkers, please call 416.531.7399 or 1.800.387.3206. Or visit *strategiccoach.com*.

The Team Success Handbook

yourteamsuccess.com

It takes a certain mindset to be able to work in an entrepreneurial structure. *The Team Success Handbook* provides the thinking tools to help team members better understand the person they're working for (usually the owner) and, from there, develop strategies to be successful and take advantage of all the unique opportunities that exist in an entrepreneurial company.

This useful guide outlines 12 success strategies for having an entrepreneurial attitude, providing the road map for a rewarding and fulfilling working career.

What's your entrepreneurial attitude aptitude? Below are the 12 strategies for success in any entrepreneurial business.

1.   Create value.
2.   Take initiative.
3.   Focus on results.
4.   Have an ownership attitude.
5.   Be in alignment.
6.   Be a partner.
7.   Take action.
8.   Be open.
9.   Communicate.
10. Learn how to handle strong emotions.
11. Have patience and compassion.
12. Don't give up.

12 Strategies For Highly Productive Entrepreneurial Teams

1. Create value.

2. Take initiative.

3. Focus on results.

4. Have an ownership attitude.

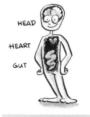

5. Be in alignment.

6. Be a partner.

7. Take action.

8. Be open.

9. Communicate.

10. Learn how to handle strong emotions.

11. Have patience and compassion.

12. Don't give up.

Acknowledgments

As with most books, this one was a team effort. First, thank you to my amazing, talented, and always gracious co-author, Jayne Stymiest. Jayne, your willingness to take on this project and create flow out of my disparate thoughts is very much appreciated. I hope you're as thrilled as I am with the end result!

Thank you to my dear friend and gifted colleague, Catherine Nomura—the writing goddess. You saw what no one else could and came to my rescue to put this book into meaningful order. Without you, it wouldn't have seen the light of day. Thank you for your friendship and partnership always.

To my creative partner and friend, Cathy Davis—I treasure our relationship, and I'm grateful every day that you choose to share your gifts and talents with me. I make it up, and you make it real—without you, very little happens! You're always encouraging me to take on my ideas, while adding your special touch, making it that much better. Thank you.

To my support partner, confidante, and the queen of scheduling, Nicole Pitcher—my life is immeasurably better since we started working together. Thank you for your gentle and loving support, and for brilliantly arranging my time so this book could happen. You're a gift in my life.

Thank you to the creative maestro, Christine Nishino. It was your jumping in that gave this project the momentum it desperately needed. Thank you, as well, to the ever-so-capable Production Team whose time and effort made this book beautiful and engaging: Suzanne Noga, Jennifer Bhatthal, Myrna Nemirsky, and Kerri Morrison.

Thank you to my internal readers and contributors for taking the time to read, add, edit, and correct mistakes. This book is so much better and richer for your input: Julia Waller, Myrna Nemirsky, Nicole Pitcher, Catherine Nomura, Karen Skleryk, Serafina Pupillo, and Tami Coville.

To my other colleagues and friends who leant their time, thinking, and expertise—Julia Waller, Paul Hamilton, Willard Bond, Jodette Janowiak, Kathy Valant, Marilyn Waller, Karen Skleryk, Eleonora Mancini, Paulette Sopoci, and Tami Coville.

To our Coach+ Team and coaches, thank you for supporting my ideas and selling and delivering the Team Programs with heart and talent: Julia Waller, Cathy Davis, Kathy Valant, Jodette Janowiak, Kristi Chambers, Paulette Sopoci, Maureen Sullivan Garrelts, Marilyn Prebul, Nicole Solitar, Tanya Voytovech, and Rebecca Powsney.

I'd also like to acknowledge my phenomenal clients, especially in The Strategic Coach® Team Leader Program. You were the first people with whom I shared this idea, and your input contributed to many of the ideas in this book.

A special mention to Sandra Wiley, Eric Sholberg, and the many other Strategic Coach clients (who'd prefer to remain anonymous) for graciously sharing your stories of "multiplication by subtraction" with me.

And also to the gracious readers who contributed invaluable input and feedback. You've made this book better!

Lastly, thank you to Dan and Babs, co-founders of Strategic Coach. You've created an environment that's allowed us to thrive, to discover and share our Unique Abilities, to experiment and create new things, and to have genuine, caring, contributing relationships with our incredible Strategic Coach clients. I love our friendship and our partnership, and I can't wait to see what the future brings.

Resources & Recommended Reading

Necessary Endings: The Employees, Businesses, and Relationships That All of Us Have to Give up in Order to Move Forward
By Dr. Henry Cloud

Delivering Happiness: A Path to Profits, Passion, and Purpose
By Tony Hsieh

The Five Dysfunctions of a Team: A Leadership Fable
By Patrick Lencioni

The Advantage: Why Organizational Health Trumps Everything Else In Business
By Patrick Lencioni

Overcoming the Five Dysfunctions of a Team: A Field Guide for Leaders, Managers, and Facilitators
By Patrick M. Lencioni

Tribal Leadership: Leveraging Natural Groups to Build a Thriving Organization
By Dave Logan, John King, and Halee Fischer-Wright

Fierce Conversations: Achieving Success at Work & in Life, One Conversation at a Time
By Susan Scott

Discovering Your Strengths

The Conative Connection: Uncovering the Link between Who You Are and How You Perform
By Kathy Kolbe

Now, Discover Your Strengths
By Marcus Buckingham and Donald O. Clifton

Strengths-Based Leadership
By Tom Rath and Barry Conchie

Discovery Tools

Affective (Personality)
StrengthsFinder
strengthsfinder.com

Cognitive (IQ)
Wonderlic
wonderlic.com

DISC: Personality Insights
personality-insights.com

Myers-Briggs
myersbriggs.org

Conative (Striving Instincts)
Kolbe
kolbe.com

For a full list of recommended reading, go to *yourteamsuccess.com*

Do You Have A Right-Fit Team Surrounding You?

As an individual, you can choose which mindsets are going to determine the structure and outcome of your entire life. This is why it's so important to surround yourself with team members who think like you do and align with your core values. Use **The Right-Fit Team Member Scorecard** to discover how engaged your team members currently are and, perhaps, where changes need to be made.

Complete the scorecard in two simple steps:
1. **Score.** Read the statements and choose the one for each category that best aligns with your current reality. When scoring your team members, be honest—for yourself and for your own growth.
2. **Improve.** Make the improvements and decisions in your business that will help you cultivate a team that's creative, productive, and thriving.

Here's to your team success!